Real Princesses

An Inside Look at Royal Life

Real Princesses

An Inside Look at Royal Life

VALERIE WILDING

WALKER & COMPANY NEW YORK

Credits

Edited by Clare Hibbert/Designed by Tinstar Design

Cover photos:
(From left to right) Reuters/Corbis. Popperfoto. Rex Features. Corbis.

Inside photos:
Alamy: 23tl. Bridgeman: 21t. Corbis: 7tl; 10; 25tc; 37r; 47; 50tl; 53bl; 53bc; 53tr.
Getty: 7cr; 8–9t; 9b; 11; 13; 16; 17t; 18; 19t; 19cl; 20; 21c; 23tc; 25br; 27; 28; 31t; 35br; 37l; 38; 43tl; 44–45; 45b; 52bl; 52br; 57; 58; 59t; 59b; 60.
Getty/National Geographic: 51tr. iStockphoto/Smiley Joanne: 5; 40; 62tl; 62bl; 63tr; 63br. iStockphoto/Stuart Pitkin: 21c frame; 26 frame; 42 frame.
iStockphoto/Nicholas Belton: 33 frame. Ministry4 of Communications, Government of Lesotho: 6. Rex: 12; 14; 15; 17b; 22–23b; 24; 25bl; 26; 29tr; 29br; 31b; 32; 33; 34; 35tl; 36; 37c; 39; 40b; 41; 42; 43bl; 46; 48; 49; 50c; 50bl; 50br; 51br; 54; 55; 56; 61t; 61b. Topfoto: 50tr.

Published in the United States of America in 2007 by
Walker Publishing Company, Inc.
Distributed to the trade by Holtzbrinck Publishers

First published in the UK in 2007 by Oxford University Press
Created by White-Thomson Publishing Ltd

For information about permission to reproduce selections from
this book, write to Permissions, Walker & Company,
104 Fifth Avenue, New York, New York 10011

Library of Congress Cataloging-in-Publication Data
available upon request
ISBN-13: 978-0-8027-9675-2 • ISBN-10: 0-8027-9675-3

Printed in Singapore by Imago
2 4 6 8 10 9 7 5 3 1

Contents

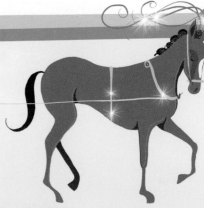

What Is a Princess?

It's the favorite dream of many girls—to be a beautiful princess, to live in a fairy-tale palace, to wear diamond tiaras, and to dress in fabulous clothes.

BUT WHAT EXACTLY IS A PRINCESS? A PRINCESS IS A member of a royal family, often the daughter or granddaughter of a king. So to be born a princess, you need the right parents.

Sometimes other members of the royal family also become princesses. A hundred years ago, Lady Alexandra Duff and her sister, Lady Maud Duff, were each given the grand title of Princess of Great Britain and Ireland by their grandfather, King Edward VII. They must have been absolutely thrilled.

PRINCESS PROFILE

Little Princess Senate's parents are the king and queen of the African country of Lesotho, so she was born a princess. When the king arrived at the hospital after Senate's birth, water was thrown at him. He didn't mind! It's a Lesotho tradition.

♠ **Princess Sayako, daughter of the Japanese emperor, gave up her title in 2005 after she married a commoner.**

♥ **Glamorous Australian Mary Donaldson met Crown Prince Frederik of Denmark in a pub in Sydney.**

S O CAN ANY GIRL BECOME A PRINCESS? IN THEORY, YES. YOU could marry a prince! And, believe it or not, you don't have to be particularly well-to-do to catch one and join him at the altar. Some unlikely people have done just that.

Some royal babies are entitled to be princesses as soon as they're born, but they never use the title. It's usually because their parents feel their daughters will be much happier if they can grow up living a normal life. If you're called "Miss," you're less likely to attract lots of attention from the newspapers and TV than if you're called "Princess."

Some girls are born princesses and, when they're old enough, decide being a princess is not for them. It's like a fairy tale in reverse. Princess Sayako, daughter of the emperor and empress of Japan, married a commoner and instantly lost her status as a princess. She's making great efforts to adjust to life as an

Marry a prince

ordinary Japanese wife, learning to drive and to shop. She'll still visit her family at the palace, though. She may no longer be a princess, but her royal relations have promised her nothing has changed. Of course, Sayako may think differently!

Top places to meet a charming prince!

In a muddy field, in your rain boots!
That's where Diana, Princess of Wales, met her prince.

At your friend's
You never know who'll show up. Letizia Ortiz met her Spanish prince at a friend's house, and love blossomed.

♛

At his college
Princess Elizabeth and her parents were visiting a naval college in Dartmouth, England, when the thirteen-year-old first laid eyes on the handsome cadet who was to become her husband. Was it love at first sight? Elizabeth, now Queen of Great Britain and Northern Ireland, isn't telling!

Ruling Lines of Europe

Most of us don't know much about our ancestors. If we want to find out more, we have to dig up family secrets from old records, letters, or maybe from the Internet.

A PRINCESS NEVER HAS TO DIG FOR SECRETS BECAUSE ROYAL family documents are carefully preserved. But if her several-times great-grandfather was less than perfect, the whole world knows about it. Nothing's private!

Princesses have their own place in line to be the next ruler. In some countries, the king or queen's oldest child is automatically first. The United Kingdom's princess royal, Anne, has been edged down the line as more brothers came along, and then nieces and nephews. When she was born she was second in line, but now she's ninth.

The kingdom of the Netherlands has had queens for over a century. The present queen is Beatrix. Her son, Prince Willem-Alexander, will succeed her. He'll be followed by his daughter, Catharina-Amalia, who was born a double princess—Princess of the Netherlands and Princess of Orange-Nassau.

THE PRINCELY HOUSE OF LIECHTENSTEIN IS ONE OF EUROPE'S oldest ruling families: it's been around for almost 1,000 years.

Why "Princely"? The head of the family is a prince or princess, not a king. Prince Hans-Adam will be followed by his son, Alois. His sister, Princess Tatjana, and

♛

Catharina-Amalia was born a double princess

daughter, Princess Marie-Caroline, won't head the family unless there's no prince available.

Prince Willem-Alexander (center) waves to the cheering Dutch people. His wife, Crown Princess Maxima, stands on his left; on his right is his mother, Queen Beatrix, all in blue.

This is one royal house where the eldest male child succeeds his father.

Another principality, Monaco, has been ruled by the Grimaldi family for 700 years. The present prince is Albert. Who's next? If Albert doesn't marry and have children, his elder sister, Princess Caroline, will become Caroline I of Monaco.

Crown Princess Victoria of Sweden belongs to a 200-year-old family called the House of Bernadotte. Victoria will become queen one day, so she has to combine royal duties with all her other interests. She sometimes stands in for her father, King Carl Gustaf, when he's away. It's good practice!

Crown Princess Victoria of Sweden attends lots of formal events, but she enjoys the outdoor life, too. She loves bees—and she knows a lot about making honey!

PRINCESS FACT
Grace Kelly was a famous movie star before she married Monaco's Prince Rainier and became Princess Grace.

PRINCESS FACT
Scottish Mary Stuart was born a princess and stayed one for just six days. Then she became queen!

African and Middle Eastern Royals

What's it like to be Miss Somebody one day, and Princess So-and-So the next? Exciting? Then just imagine having two new titles ...

PRINCESS LALLA SALMA HAS THREE SISTERS-IN-LAW: LALLA MERYEM, Lalla Asma, and Lalla Hasna.

Hold on! Four princesses with the same first name? No! "Lalla" just means "Lady," so the name after Lalla is the princess's real one. Lalla Salma is the wife of King Mohammed VI of Morocco. He's the latest ruler of the royal House of Alaoui. So who's next? Princess Lalla Salma's son, little Crown Prince Moulay Hassan, is all set to succeed his father.

Red-haired Princess Lalla Salma is the first wife of a Moroccan king to be given the title "princess."

Probably the most famous African princess is Elizabeth of Toro, Uganda. In 1966, her

In the 1960s the UK's Princess Margaret invited Elizabeth of Toro to model in a charity fashion show. Elizabeth was so beautiful that she went on to have a career as a supermodel. She now works hard to help the Ugandan people.

family's reign came to an end when the monarchy was abolished. After years of strife in her homeland, Elizabeth eventually saw the monarchy restored. She became the Batebe (First Lady) of Toro and guardian to the infant King Oyo.

THE HASHEMITE FAMILY OF JORDAN IS RICH IN PRINCESSES! King Abdullah has two princes and two princesses, Iman and Salma. He has seven sisters—all princesses— and four brothers. Some of those have had little princesses, too! Who'll be the next king? It's likely to be Prince Hussein, the king's eldest son.

The king and queen of the African country of Lesotho have two children, Princess Senate and her little sister, Princess 'MaSeeiso. Only males can succeed to the throne, so the princesses' uncle, Prince Seeiso, is next in line. But there's talk of changing the law, so who knows—maybe one day Senate will be queen.

🔥 **Jordan's Princess Noor is married to Crown Prince Hamzah, the king's half-brother. "Noor" is also her mother-in-law's name. It means "light."**

Ruling Lines of Asia

Most little girls dream of what they'll be when they grow up. As long as it's not a fairy or a Martian, they can probably become anything they want.

♥ Princess Aiko sits on her mother's knee, next to Emperor Akihito. The two younger princesses behind the emperor and empress are Aiko's cousins, Mako and Kako.

BUT JAPANESE PRINCESSES IN THE PAST HAVE ALWAYS HAD THEIR futures pretty well mapped out for them—until now. The Japanese royal family traces its ancestors back nearly 1,500 years. The

One day Aiko might become empress of Japan

present monarch is Emperor Akihito. His son, Crown Prince Naruhito, is next in line for the

Crown Princess Himani is married to Crown Prince Paras of Nepal. They have three children: Princess Purnika, Prince Hridayendra, and Princess Kritika.

PRINCESS FACT
Crown Prince Naruhito proposed three times before Masako agreed to become his princess.

PRINCESS TEASER
Why did almost 1,000 plainclothes police officers surround Mickey Mouse? Answer on page 64.

PRINCESS TEASER
Which dinosaur was named after a princess? Answer on page 64.

Chrysanthemum Throne of Japan. But who will follow him?

Naruhito and his wife, Crown Princess Masako, have one daughter, Princess Aiko, who was born in 2001. There was talk of changing the law so that princesses could have equal rights to inherit the throne, but in September 2006, a son, Prince Hisahito, was born to Naruhito's younger brother and his wife. Hisahito jumps ahead of little Aiko and becomes third in line to the throne.

KING BHUMIBOL, OF THAILAND'S ROYAL HOUSE OF CHAKRI, is currently the longest-reigning monarch in the world. He and his wife, Queen Sirikit, have four children: a boy and three girls. Crown Prince Vajiralongkorn will step ahead of his older sister to succeed his father.

Vajiralongkorn is married to Princess Srirasmi. One of his sisters, Princess Sirindhorn, is a whizz at Information Technology! Another, Princess Chulabhorn, is a scientist, and she has two princesses of her own: Siribhachudhabhorn and Adityadornkitikhun. It must not have been easy for them to learn to write their names!

A few years ago, the king, queen, and seven other members of the Nepalese royal family were tragically killed. Prince Gyanendra suddenly, and unexpectedly, found himself king—the latest ruler of the Himalayan Kingdom of Nepal's Shah dynasty.

Something pink, something blue...

...Hop off frog, I'm not kissing you!

Family

Imagine you're a princess. You're fourteen, and you're being sent abroad to marry a complete stranger. Now imagine there's no phone and no e-mail, and letters take weeks to arrive...

THIS WAS THE FATE OF SPANISH PRINCESS ANNE OF AUSTRIA, SENT TO marry fourteen-year-old King Louis XIII of France. The marriage had been arranged so France and Spain would unite against their enemies. Anne was miserable at first, though things did improve—for a while. But when France declared war on Anne's homeland, Spain, she must have felt the marriage had been for nothing. Nowadays, most princesses hope to marry for love, but it wasn't always so. In the past, most royal marriages were about bringing countries together. A princess was lucky if she found love—but it did happen.

♦ **Welsh princess Caroline Matilda was only fifteen when she was sent to marry the king of Denmark. She was unhappy throughout her marriage and died at age twenty-three.**

In 1540 Anne of Cleves married the English king, Henry VIII. The marriage didn't last, but she remained a princess of England for the rest of her life.

FRENCH PRINCESS HENRIETTA MARIA, SENT TO ENGLAND IN 1625 to marry King Charles I, brought lots of servants with her. The king didn't like paying for their upkeep and sent most of them home. Henrietta Maria was livid! The king's behavior caused a major argument between the newlyweds. Eventually, they began to care for each other, and soon this fondness deepened to love.

ANNE OF CLEVES SAILED TO ENGLAND to become King Henry VIII's fourth wife. He had a falling out with the pope, leaving his country rather lonely among Europe's many Catholic countries.

Anne's marriage strengthened England's links with the Protestant duchy of Cleves, but it lasted only six months! Henry is said to have nicknamed poor Anne the "Flanders Mare"—because he thought she looked ugly.

After her marriage ended Anne made the best of life in her new land. The king treated her as his sister, called her "princess," and gave her money and beautiful homes.

PRINCESS FACT

Portugal's Catherine of Braganza introduced tea drinking to England.

Getting married? Worries for princesses past...

♛ **Have you met your future husband? He might be older than your father— or younger than you!**

♛ *Will you ever see your family again? It'll take weeks or months to reach your new land. You can't run home for lunch with Mom.*

♛ **Will your new family like you? They might think that new hairstyle's peculiar or laugh at your clothes. You're fashionable here, but over there . . .**

♛ *Will they understand you? You can't speak their language! How will you ask where to find the bathroom?*

Traditional or Modern?

Are princesses' families the same the world over? Not at all. Some are very wealthy and have a lavish lifestyle, while others live more simply.

A PRINCESS'S FATHER MAY NOT BE A KING OR A PRINCE. HE MIGHT be a sultan or an emir. Once, he might have been an Egyptian pharaoh or an Indian maharaja. Princess Elizabeth of Toro's father was an *omukama*, and a Chinese princess might have been the daughter of a *huangdi*. The father of Princess Alexandra of Luxembourg is a grand duke who rules a grand duchy, rather than a kingdom.

The way royal families live is different. Some may have a number of palaces; others have just one. Some mix freely with their people; others are aloof.

The Dutch royal family is sometimes nicknamed the "bicycling monarchy." Like millions of people in the

Some have a relaxed, low-key style of monarchy

Netherlands, the queen's mother, Juliana, used to love riding around on her bike. Belgium's Princess

The Norwegian royals may be relaxed, but Mette-Marit still has to look the part. She's really put on some bling for this state banquet!

Three wheels for two princesses! Little Elisabeth of Belgium pedals hard behind her mom, Mathilde, as they cycle along a wooded lane.

Mathilde enjoys cycling with her family, too, but that's not the reason her family is also known as a "bicycling monarchy." And it's not because they can't afford cars, either—the Belgian royals are pretty wealthy. The reason is that, like the Dutch, they have a relaxed, low-key style of monarchy—not showy or pretentious.

BRITAIN'S ROYALS ARE VERY FORMAL. THERE ARE MANY EVENTS throughout the year involving family members, such as trooping the color, the state opening of parliament, and receptions for

Anne, the UK's Princess Royal, wears the uniform of Colonel of the Blues and Royals as she takes part in a big parade known as trooping the color.

visiting heads of state. These are formal, precision-planned occasions—not particularly relaxing for anybody!

The younger princes and princesses occasionally let their hair down—and hit the headlines!—but are still quite removed from everyday British life. Sophie, Prince Edward's wife, kept her job for a while when she married, but she's now deep into royal duties.

Different days for different princesses!

Princess Isabella

7:00 am *Send for servant to walk dogs*

9:00 am *Choose pony bridle*

9:15 am *Ballroom dancing*

10:15 am *Inspect regiment; present medals*

12:00 pm *Luncheon with Daddy and the prime minister*

2:00 pm *Dressmaker*

2:30 pm *Dictate letters*

3:50 pm *Tour school for the visually impaired*

4:45 pm *Open youth theater*

7:00 pm *Reception and dinner for foreign guests*

Princess Izzy

8:00 am *Walk the dogs*

9:00 am *Buy new nose stud*

10:00 am *Yoga class*

11:30 am *Download music for great new iPod*

12:30 pm *Lunch: Poverty Action Focus Group*

2:30 pm *Shopping!*

4:00 pm *Open children's hospice, stay a while*

5:30 pm *Catch up on soaps*

7:00 pm *Dinner with Mom and Dad*

8:30 pm *Out clubbing!*

Do All Princesses Become Queen?

Being a princess doesn't automatically mean you'll rule one day. Some do, some don't, some will, some won't!

♥ **Princess Salote of Tonga was spoiled as a child. Her attendants often carried her, so she didn't walk where common people walked. She became queen at eighteen.**

SOME PRINCESSES BECOME QUEEN IF THEY'RE THE ELDEST child and if females in their country can inherit the throne. Sweden's seventeenth-century Princess Christina was an only child when her father was killed in battle. She was crowned queen at five years old.

Hatshepsut, princess of ancient Egypt, couldn't really help becoming queen. She was the daughter of Pharaoh Thutmose I and, when he died, she married the man who took the throne, Thutmose II. He just happened to be her half brother, and when *he* died, Hatshepsut ruled on behalf of Thutmose III—her nephew *and* stepson! She eventually had herself crowned pharaoh

---

♛

Hatshepsut had herself crowned pharaoh

---

and became one of the best "kings" Egypt ever had!

SOME PRINCESSES WON'T BE QUEENS, EVER. PERHAPS THEIR laws don't allow them to be, or maybe there's an older sister or brother who'll get there first.

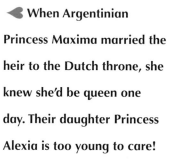

When Argentinian Princess Maxima married the heir to the Dutch throne, she knew she'd be queen one day. Their daughter Princess Alexia is too young to care!

PRINCESS TEASER
Who went up a tree as a princess and came down as a queen? Answer on page 64.

Little Princess Alexia's older sister, Catharina-Amalia, will follow her father to the Dutch throne. But Princess Alexia could still be a monarch! She might marry a crown prince and become his queen. She'd have to move to another country, though.

A few years ago, a Belgian princess would have had to make way for her younger brothers, but the law has changed to allow an older princess to wear the crown. Princess Mathilde's young daughter, Elisabeth, is already learning that one day she will be queen.

In some countries, where the law stops princesses being crowned, many people think it's unfair. Lesotho is one country where there may soon be a change, and others may follow. Little princesses may be wondering "Will I? Won't I?"

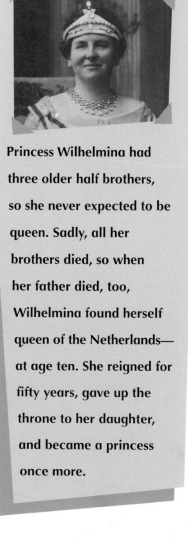

PRINCESS PROFILE

Princess Wilhelmina had three older half brothers, so she never expected to be queen. Sadly, all her brothers died, so when her father died, too, Wilhelmina found herself queen of the Netherlands—at age ten. She reigned for fifty years, gave up the throne to her daughter, and became a princess once more.

19

A Real Princess?

There seem to be a lot of princesses out there, but are they real princesses? What about all those princesses from countries that don't have a monarchy anymore?

CERTIFIED ROYAL

Princess Maria-Olympia of Greece is also a princess of Denmark. That's because one of her grandmothers was a Danish princess.

WHEN ROYAL FAMILIES ARE PUT OUT OF THE BUSINESS OF reigning, they're usually expected to leave their homeland—whether they want to or not! It's often too dangerous to stay. The new government wouldn't want a king around, rallying people to restore him to the throne.

When the Greek monarchy was abolished in 1974, the government discouraged King Constantine from returning, but now he's allowed to visit Greece when he wants. His granddaughter, Princess Maria-Olympia, was born in America.

SOME PRINCESSES DON'T HAVE A DROP OF ROYAL BLOOD. THAT'S BECAUSE they're fakes! Mary Carleton decided it might be profitable to tell people she was a German princess. They believed her! She cheated several men out of money and beautiful clothes and was eventually hanged. Harsh punishment? This was the seventeenth century.

More recently, an American woman posed as a Saudi princess and went on a wild shopping

CERTIFIED FAKE

A girl wearing strange, Asian-style clothes was found wandering English lanes in 1817. Her name was Caraboo, and she spoke no English.

Using an interpreter, she explained that she had escaped from kidnappers and was an Eastern princess. True? No. Princess Caraboo was plain Mary Baker—a servant!

spree. When caught cheating an insurance company, she blamed the credit-card company for allowing her to spend so much!

POCAHONTAS ISN'T JUST A DISNEY CHARACTER— SHE WAS A REAL-LIFE Native American girl who's said to have saved the life of a seventeenth-century Englishman. Later, she married a tobacco planter named John Rolfe, who took her to England. Pocahontas was welcomed into London society. Before long, people began to call this chief's lively daughter "Princess Pocahontas."

Daughter of a Powhatan Chief, Pocahontas was presented to King James I and the rest of the royal family.

Living in a Palace

Palace! The word conjures up pictures of ballrooms, banquet halls, and bedrooms with four-poster beds... Is it really like that? In most cases, yes.

CROWN PRINCESS SARAH, THE TEENAGE WIFE OF THE CROWN PRINCE OF BRUNEI, must have been blown away when she first explored her future home. The golden-domed Nurul Iman Palace has more than 1,780 rooms! At least 250 are bathrooms: that's an awful lot of toilets to clean! Luckily the Brunei royal family is extremely wealthy and can afford hundreds of servants. Princess Sarah's father-in-law is said to own more than 150 Rolls Royce cars. And if he gets fed up traveling by road, he can always take off in one of his private planes. Or helicopters...

In many palaces, lots of the rooms are used as offices and for

➤ **Brunei's Nurul Iman Palace is probably the world's largest royal residence. It boasts five swimming pools!**

➤ **Princess Grace of Monaco lived in the Prince's Palace, which has spectacular views of the Mediterranean.**

official entertaining. Include the kitchens, laundries, and all the servants' quarters, and there's not much living space left for the

royal family. But Princess Sarah's palace is first and foremost the royal residence. She can ask 5,000 guests to dinner—and fit them all in!

———— ♛ ————

The Nurul Iman Palace has more than 1,780 rooms

THE PRINCE'S PALACE IN THE TINY COASTAL PRINCIPALITY OF MONACO must have one of the most spectacular settings of any royal home. The former fortress is perched high over the sea and has a view of the blue Mediterranean on three sides. In spite of its rather severe appearance, the palace is full of beautiful features. Its inner courtyard is paved with colored pebbles—three million of them—laid out in a geometric pattern that centers on twin curved marble staircases.

It's great living in a palace… Or is it?

♛

♛ **You can have any fancy food you like…but you can't run out for a burger.**

♛ *You have the most beautiful bedroom imaginable…but you can't have friends visit for a sleepover.*

♛ **Want a pair of pink suede boots? You can have them…but you can't go and buy them yourself.**

♛ *If you're hungry in the middle of the night, you can send for food…but you can't raid the fridge and make a peanut butter and jelly sandwich.*

♛ **You've got lots of new CDs…but you can't drop by to share them with your best friend.**

♛ *You're on your own, princess!*

Princesses Without Palaces

Does every princess have a fairy-tale palace? Not at all. Many are brought up in more ordinary homes, and some princesses have lived in terrible surroundings.

PRINCESS TEASER

Which princess was locked up in the Tower of London? Answer on page 64.

PRINCESS ELIZABETH, LATER QUEEN ELIZABETH II, SPENT HER EARLY YEARS in a house in Piccadilly, London. It might not have been a palace, but the house had twenty-five bedrooms, and the tiny princess had her very own nursery suite.

Even though Elizabeth's granddaughters, Princess Beatrice and Princess Eugenie, are fifth and sixth in line to the throne, they've never lived in palaces. As children, their home was brand-new Sunninghill Park. Still, it had a dozen bedrooms!

Exiled families, like the Greek royals, must live where they can. At least the Greeks had the rest of the world to choose from. In the late thirteenth century, poor Gwenllian, a Welsh princess, was seen as a threat to the English throne. She was locked up for the rest of her life—another fifty-three years!

Indian Wilayat Mahal claimed she was a princess whose family had lost its power and wealth.

◀ **When Princess Beatrice had a birthday party at Sunninghill Park, she didn't go to the fair— it came to her!**

With her two children, five servants, and twelve dogs, she went to live on a railway platform. It took her nine years to force the government to give them a home. Now her children live in a large, but decaying, house.

MANY MODERN PRINCESSES MOVE AWAY FROM THE palace to study. An ordinary girl in college gets used to a tiny dorm room or a shared house. A student princess, even with a whole apartment or house to herself, must also adapt to simpler surroundings. No doubt she'll take a few little luxuries with her! All these temporary homes, we can be sure, have to be pretty special.

Japan's Princess Chichibu never forgot sleeping in a tent with her prince and princess cousins after a massive earthquake in 1923. With nowhere else to go, the family set up home in some sewage pipes.

♥ Crown Princess Marie-Chantal of Greece, in white, knew there'd be no palace upbringing for her new baby daughter. The family lives in exile.

♥ Princess Madeleine of Sweden stayed with friends in London while she was studying English. It meant she could live like an ordinary person for a while.

25

No School!

Being a princess means never having to go to school, right? Not necessarily! Everybody needs an education—and that includes princesses.

PRINCESSES HAVEN'T ALWAYS HAD TO LEARN THE SAME KINDS OF THINGS. A medieval princess didn't need to know anything about furnishing a palace. After all, you can do only so much with stone walls and a tapestry. She needed skills to help pass the time in a world without paperbacks or TV. Her mother taught her to embroider or stitch tapestries. She had a dancing instructor and learned to sing. Music instructors taught her to play the lute or, like sixteenth-century Princess Margaret, an early form of keyboard called the clavichord.

♠ A typical day for Princess Elizabeth was Greek all morning and Latin all afternoon—and she still found time to write her own music. She became a great queen as Elizabeth I of England!

PRINCESS FACT
More than 3,000 years after Hatshepsut's death, an asteroid was named after her.

PRINCESS AMINA OF ZAZZAU, A SIXTEENTH-CENTURY KINGDOM IN Nigeria, was taught to fight as well as run a household. With her great knowledge of battle tactics, she kept her land strong and powerful.

Inca princess Chimpu Ocllo learned the history of her people, as well as all the skills needed by sixteenth-century Inca women, such as spinning and weaving.

Life was very different for Anglo-Saxon princess Aethelburh, who was sent to a nunnery to be educated. She must have been

———— ♕ ————

Princess Amina was taught to fight

a good worker, because she ended up not as a princess or a queen but a saint! Four of Aethelburh's sisters were named saints, too!

Henry VIII's daughter, Princess Elizabeth, later Elizabeth I of England, was an intelligent girl who had excellent teachers and loved to study. Before she'd even reached her teens, she was an ace at Latin and was making terrific progress in Italian and French.

◄ **Egyptian princess Hatshepsut's father made sure she learned about art and architecture. When she grew up, Hatshepsut commissioned fancy buildings and beautiful statues.**

It must have been great not going to school... right?

♕

♕ *No school bus to catch! Great! Bad news: the lessons were in your home.*

♕ **Only one teacher. Hooray! Bad news: he watched you all the time.**

♕ *No school uniform. Cool! Bad news: every day was dress-up day.*

♕ **No school bully. Good! Bad news: no friends, either.**

♕ *No school lunches. Yum! Bad news: boring meal with tutor.*

♕ **No smelly locker rooms. Phew! Bad news: exercise in long skirt and petticoats.**

♕ *No end-of-year exams! Excellent! Bad news: no end-of-year dance, either.*

A day in the life of a princess's teacher

Princess Tina's father brought her to school today. I hate that. Curtsying makes my knees creak. At morning break I investigated a noise in the bathroom. Tina's friends were trying on her mother's tiara. I confiscated it immediately! I couldn't resist trying it on, though. I was glittering!

The bodyguards keep moaning that the chairs they sit on outside the door are too small. One broke his chair today—the third this semester—so I made him sit on the floor, legs crossed, arms folded. The poor man was livid!

The guards eat so much, too! Four children had no lunch today because those oafs had three helpings each. Now I must write to the king about Princess Tina's homework—he keeps doing it for her, and unfortunately he gets all the answers wrong.

A Normal Education?

Today's princesses don't have to study all alone in a stuffy palace schoolroom while ordinary girls play sports and go on class trips. Modern princesses get to join in, too!

CROWN PRINCESS MASAKO OF JAPAN WANTS HER DAUGHTER, PRINCESS Aiko, to enjoy the things that other children do. Aiko goes on outings to places like the zoo, and now she's started school. She was just as nervous as any little girl when she entered kindergarten, but she soon settled down. She loves to paint and make a mess, and now she has lots of friends to play with!

A princess has to pay attention in class, especially if she might one day be queen. Like it or not, she'll need to know at least one

♥ **Princess Aiko walks to school with her parents—just like any ordinary little girl. The difference is that one day her father will be emperor of Japan!**

28

foreign language—maybe more. That's because she'll meet a lot of foreign people, and it's no good if everyone shakes hands then looks at each other with nothing to say! She'll need a sound knowledge of her country's history, too. That'll give her something to talk about during state visits.

$\mathcal{P}$RINCESS MARGRETHE OF DENMARK STUDIED EMBROIDERY and art, as well as all the usual subjects, at her fancy private school. That early training paid off. Margrethe, now queen, is a terrific artist. She draws, paints, illustrates books, and even designs costumes for TV and film productions.

▶ As Belgium's Princess Elisabeth is carried to school, she has her bright new backpack and a fun day with friends ahead of her. What more could a little princess want?

Thoroughly modern princesses Beatrice and Eugenie of York have both attended several British schools. Eugenie is at a co-ed boarding school. Beatrice, who overcame dyslexic problems to get great grades, is already planning her college years—which might be spent in America!

▶ Princess Caroline had a varied education: first with a governess at the palace in Monaco, then at a convent school, an English boarding school, and finally a Paris university. She speaks many languages fluently!

CALAMARI SNAILS OYSTERS FROGS' LEGS

Food Fit for a Princess

If a princess craves a banana split with chocolate chip ice cream and raspberry sauce, she only has to ask. It will be delivered to her with a cherry on top!

EVERY PALACE HAS A HUGE KITCHEN FULL OF TOP CHEFS WHO'VE been trained to produce food fit for royalty—but that doesn't mean that princesses can eat whatever they want. Even palace food has its drawbacks. For one thing, a princess's apartment might be a long way from the kitchen, so her scrambled eggs on toast turn into a cold, solid mess by the time they reach her.

In the past, there was always the danger that someone might want to poison the royal family. Enter the food taster! He sampled a mouthful of each dish, and the royals had to wait a few minutes to make sure he was okay and that the meal was safe to eat. Cold food again! (Or a dead taster and no dinner…)

THE UPSIDE OF BEING ROYAL IS THAT YOU GET TO EAT WONDERFUL FOOD. After all, there's a long tradition of sumptuous dishes being set before the king and his family. However, today's princesses would probably pass out at the sight of a medieval

♛

Live birds flew out of a pie

royal dinner. There used to be forty or fifty different dishes—and one specialty was live birds that flew out of a pie!

It's important that a princess shows respect to other people's customs.

So from an early age she's trained to eat what's put in front of her, whether she likes it or not. One day, perhaps in a foreign land, she might be presented with something that may be disgusting to her but that's a special delicacy to the people she's visiting. It would be a great insult if she were to turn up her royal nose!

 Denmark's Crown Princess Mary was a guest at this feast in Hamburg, Germany. A place setting at a big function can be daunting, but Mary has attended so many royal banquets that she knows just when to use each piece of silverware and crystal glassware.

 There can't be many cakes like this one, made to celebrate the baptism of Italian princess Maria Carolina. It's shaped like one of Italy's best-known landmarks—the volcano Vesuvius!

A Princess in Sneakers?

Do princesses always have to dress up? No, they don't. After all, they're not always on display. But when they are, they have to get it right.

EVEN A PRINCESS IS ALLOWED TO BE HERSELF NOW AND again, and that's when she lets her hair down and wears the clothes *she* wants to wear. Spot a princess on vacation and she's likely to be wearing the same sort of thing as you—maybe jeans and sneakers, or a T-shirt and cutoffs. Her hair's probably casual, and her understated jewelry won't exactly dazzle you.

◀ **Like her mom, Princess Caroline, Charlotte of Monaco manages to look stylish in whatever she's wearing, whether it's riding pants, a ski suit— or her favorite pair of jeans.**

32

But when a princess is out in public—whether on a low-key trip to the circus or attending a fancy state reception—she pulls out all the stops. Every little detail will be considered and planned, from the right shoes to the choice of hat or tiara. A princess can't afford to make mistakes. If she does, pictures of her fashion disaster will be splashed across the newspapers.

PRINCESSES NEED OUTFITS FOR ALL SORTS OF OCCASIONS. PRINCESS Haya of Jordan leads a full life, so any normal day might mean several changes of clothes. She'll begin in a swimsuit or sweatpants for her exercise, then change into riding gear to work with her horses. Lunchtime means a change into something clean, then perhaps a dash to her room to put on a nice suit for one of her charity meetings. Back into riding pants for one last ride, and then, if she has guests, she must slip into a beautiful gown for the evening.

Most princesses have a dresser to help them choose the right outfit, whether it's a pretty dress for a ship launching, a safari suit for visiting a village project in the developing world, or a floor-sweeping ball gown, glistening with pearls and silver embroidery.

▲ **Special outfits for two Italian princesses! Proud mom Camilla wears a pretty pink suit, while baby Maria Chiara wears a traditional white christening gown.**

Royal tour packing list

- **Formal dresses and jackets**
- *Umbrella for lady-in-waiting to hold over me*
- **Fancy outfits for lots of fancy affairs**
- *Jewels, including a tiara or two*
- **Hats—ugh!**
- *Black outfit in case someone dies*
- **Flat shoes for walks**
- *Boots for rough ground*
- **Heels for receptions**
- *Glittery, strappy shoes for parties—yesss!*
- **Ski suit? I should be so lucky . . .**
- *Jeans and sneakers—I might get a day on my own*
- **Bikini, in case I find a beach that day**
- *And my killer sparkly top and cutoffs for strutting on the sand*

33

Designer Dresses!

A dress for a princess must be special. So who does she turn to? Top designers, of course! And she can afford the best…

Give us a clue!
Questions for
royal designers
to ask…

An elegant dress for a family wedding? Should I insert a secret pocket for the royal confetti?

A gown for a banquet? Should I put elastic in the waist—in case your highness can't resist two helpings of dessert?

A suit for a ship launching? Should I weight the hem—in case a gust of wind exposes the royal underwear?

Jeans for days off? Would your highness like me to slash holes in the knees?

A hat for the races? Should I decorate it with fresh fruit—in case you get hungry?

A PRINCESS NEEDS A WARDROBE (OR SEVERAL WARDROBES!) full of beautiful clothes. Many will be for official wear, but if she longs for a pair of expensive designer jeans for a weekend away with friends, she can have them.

Even royal wardrobes can only house just so many outfits. Some princesses take care not to be seen twice in the same suit or dress: they give their clothes away, or even auction them. That was the fate of dresses belonging to both Diana, Princess of Wales, and Princess Lilian of Belgium.

♥ This star-spangled gown was one of seventy-nine dresses that Diana, Princess of Wales, put up for auction in New York. They raised over $3 million for charity!

Ignoring the rain, Princess Victoria of Sweden wears a stunning pink gown and fringe tiara for the wedding of Princess Anna zu Sayn-Wittgenstein-Berleburg.

PRINCESS TEASER
Which rebellious royal designer married a former fishmonger then a circus performer? Answer on page 64.

until they were asked to make the wedding dress for Diana, Princess of Wales. Suddenly they were hot news!

One designer, delighted to be asked to design for a princess, has no need of the publicity. Princess Letizia of Spain chose Manuel Pertegaz to make her wedding dress. He's designed for many famous people, and he isn't too worried about his future career—after all, he's in his 80s!

Some princesses have tried designing for themselves. Princess Stephanie of Monaco worked for Christian Dior for a while, then she put her experience to good use by designing and marketing her own collection of swimwear.

Other princesses, like Mette-Marit of Norway, have a practical approach. She'll happily reuse an outfit that everyone's seen before. Madeleine of Sweden has a down-to-earth attitude toward clothes, too—and no wonder! She looks just as gorgeous in a store-bought outfit as in a costly designer gown.

A FASHION DESIGNER CAN BE ALMOST UNKNOWN ONE DAY and world famous the next. Dressing a princess gives a great boost to a designer's career! David and Elizabeth Emanuel weren't exactly household names

Less is more! Princess Sayako of Japan arrives at Tokyo's Imperial Palace in a deceptively simple pale green gown and hat, highlighted with pearls.

Jewelry

Jewels a princess wouldn't want to own...

The Hope diamond weighs 45 carats. Legend says it was cursed when it was stolen from an Indian statue. The stone was blamed for the death of Queen Marie Antoinette in the French Revolution. It's now in the Smithsonian Natural History Museum. After all, no princess would want it hanging around her neck!

An even larger diamond, the 67.5-carat Black Orlov, belongs to a U.S. businessman. It, too, was said to carry a curse because it was stolen from an Indian statue. Two of its owners, Russian princesses Leonila and Nadia, committed suicide. Maybe princesses should avoid black diamonds! Luckily, they're incredibly rare.

PRINCESSES AREN'T SHORT OF SPARKLY BRACELETS, NECKLACES, OR RINGS. Many of them inherit magnificent family jewels the second they are born.

Of course, a baby princess is too small to wear great-grandmama's six-row pearl choker, but it'll be there for her to wear when she grows up, just as her mother used it before her.

When princesses celebrate their birthdays, relatives and friends might wonder what on earth to buy a girl who has everything. The answer? Jewelry! A princess can never have too much! After all, she can't show up at public engagements in the same old necklace, year after year.

Princess Michael of Kent's strapless black dress sets off her stunning jewelry. The dazzling tiara mirrors the curve of her matching seven-strand necklace.

WHAT MAKES A PRINCESS REALLY STAND OUT FROM the rest of the girls is her tiara. Sometimes, the first she ever owns is given to her on the day that she, an ordinary girl, marries her prince. The king and queen of Belgium gave a costly antique tiara to their new daughter-in-law, Princess Claire, when she married Prince Laurent. She certainly sparkled on the day!

Jewels don't just help a princess look glamorous. They show that her family's wealthy. A

A princess can never have too much jewelry

glittering royal family is a powerful image that says, "Our country is rich and successful."

African princess and artist Francina Ndimande wears metal rings and huge beaded hoops around her neck, long earrings, and a beaded headpiece. More hoops of tiny beads circle her ankles. These bold adornments are traditional in her Ndebele culture.

🔹 Princess Madeleine of Sweden wears a delicate necklace and coordinating earrings, with a favorite tiara adding sparkle to her hair.

🔹 Like many girls, Alexandra of Denmark has a favorite pair of earrings. She's added a necklace with a matching single giant pearl, and crowned her outfit with a glittering tiara.

PRINCESS FACT
When Elizabeth Tudor had decorated all of her fingers, she put rings in her hair!

Is It All Fun?

A lot of the time its fun being a princess. After all, the world's there for you to see and explore, and you can afford to do it.

IF YOU WANT TO TAKE UP SOME SORT OF SPORT, YOU CAN BUY THE BEST equipment and hire the best trainers. If, like Princess Caroline of Monaco and her daughter Charlotte, you love to ski, you can either head for the snowy Alps or waterski in the warm Mediterranean.

A special birthday? You could invite your favorite pop stars to come and sing for you. They'll almost certainly say yes!

Maybe you'd like to learn to fly a plane, drive a tank—or even dance in front of your prince as Diana, Princess of Wales, did! She

♛

Princess Diana danced on a London stage!

rehearsed in secret and performed on a London stage with world-famous ballet dancer Wayne Sleep. She surprised everyone—especially Prince Charles!

IF YOU WANT TO TAKE UP PHOTOGRAPHY, YOU WON'T NEED TO SAVE UP for a top-notch camera. Princesses have been talented photographers almost since cameras were invented. The British royal archives have forty albums of photos dating from 1887 taken by just one princess—Victoria, daughter of King Edward VII!

When you're not short of money, collecting can be a rewarding pastime. In the nineteenth century, Princess

PRINCESS TEASER
Which princess competed against her husband in a sailing match—and won?
Answer on page 64.

◀ Naval officer Prince Andrew's former wife, Sarah, learned to fly a helicopter. It allowed her to share one of Andrew's many interests.

▶ The music's great! Crown Princess Mette-Marit can't stay in her seat and bops the night away at a Norwegian concert.

Alexandra of Denmark and her sister Princess Dagmar, who became a Russian czarina (empress), were both rather interested in the work of Russian jeweler Peter Carl Fabergé. He became famous for his Easter eggs, intricately decorated with precious gems. Alexandra's descendants have added to her Fabergé egg collection—and today it's worth a fortune!

Princesses can indulge almost any interest, be it painting, drawing, or music. They'll have some of the finest instruments in the world—no practicing on out-of-tune old pianos for them!

PRINCESS TEASER
Which princesses' mom wrote books about a helicopter named Budgie? Answer on page 64.

Perks for a princess…

👑 **Comfortable travel: first class all the way in plane, train—and carriage.**

👑 *The best concert seats: no trying to see over someone's huge hat.*

👑 **Great vacations: visits to exotic locations, gorgeous islands, and friends' yachts…**

👑 *Hungry? Ring the bell and someone will pander to your every whim.*

👑 **No housework: just step out of your clothes and let the maid pick them up.**

👑 *Your own hairdresser: no bad hair days.*

👑 **No need to miss a World Cup Final—they'd love you to present the trophy.**

👑 *Want a new handbag? Get the store to bring a selection to the palace.*

👑 **No need to stand in line: especially for the bathroom.**

So Being Royal Is Easy?

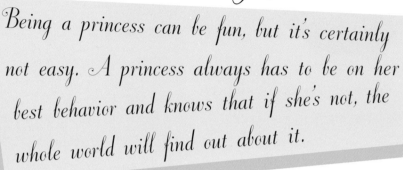

Being a princess can be fun, but it's certainly not easy. A princess always has to be on her best behavior and knows that if she's not, the whole world will find out about it.

IMAGINE BEING THE MAIN TOPIC OF CONVERSATION EVERYWHERE! IF A PRINCESS makes mistakes in what she wears, she soon earns a reputation as a fashion disaster.

And if she behaves badly just once, it won't be forgotten. Princess Stephanie of Monaco had to work hard to make up for the wild behavior of her youth. Being a princess often means

doing things you're not crazy about—or even stuff that makes you look silly. Whatever the event, you still have to look as if you'd rather be there than anywhere else in the world. Keep smiling!

THINGS ORDINARY GIRLS TAKE FOR GRANTED CAN BE ORDEALS FOR princesses. *Your* test scores are just between your family and your teachers. But if you're a princess, failing some of your tests could make headlines!

New boyfriend? *You* just have to endure your mom saying, "I don't think much of him"—but a princess has to put up with the

Before Princess Märtha Louise got married, she took part in a Norwegian princess test. Wearing a plastic crown, she had to kiss a frog. Up popped her future husband!

whole nation expressing an opinion. People will be asking: "Is he good enough?" and "Would he be a credit to the monarchy?" All these questions demand answers—never mind that the relationship might be over in a week.

A princess must keep a stiff upper lip

And if she is dumped, a princess must keep a stiff upper lip. Royals try not to show their emotions—even at funerals.

PRINCESS FACT

Princess Margaret once mingled with the cheering crowd outside London's Buckingham Palace—unrecognized!

A princess must keep a watchful eye for paparazzi—photographers who lurk in trees and behind garbage cans with telephoto lenses. If she's playing tennis at a friend's country home, she knows someone might be waiting to photograph her as she lunges for a ball and crashes into the fence.

A princess can afford gorgeous things, but can she go shopping alone? It's risky. Apart from the fact that she'd probably be surrounded by photographers in an instant, there's always the risk that someone might try to kidnap her and hold her for ransom.

Dutch Princess Catharina-Amalia finds a family day out on the Austrian ski slopes somewhat exhausting. Who can blame her for that huge yawn?

Princess dos and don'ts

DO take your friends to restaurants. DON'T order pasta. You'll be photographed with spaghetti hanging out of your mouth.

DO dress carefully. DON'T think "No one will notice that hole under my arm." They will.

DO go horseback riding. DON'T fall off. The whole world will see you face-down in the mud.

DO write a diary. DON'T ever let it out of your bedroom. It's pure media dynamite!

DO invite your friends to the palace. DON'T let them wander off on their own. They'll get either lost or arrested.

DO write love letters to your boyfriend. DON'T leave them lying around. They'll be tomorrow's hot gossip!

"I Can Do What I Want!"

The Princesse de Lamballe was the best friend of Queen Marie Antoinette. When she refused to betray the queen during the French Revolution, the crowd cut off her head.

Oh no, you can't! Being a princess doesn't mean you're above the law. What would the world be like if princesses drove sports cars over the speed limit through their cities?

SOME PRINCESSES IN THE PAST APPEARED TO BE SAFE FROM ALL HARM, like Taiping and Youlan, both from China.

Taiping was a beautiful, powerful eighth-century princess who had a close relationship with her nephew. Together, they fought to ensure their family would rule China. However, when that nephew became emperor, he feared that Taiping was too powerful. She was sentenced to death but allowed to die with honor by committing suicide.

Less than 100 years ago, being a princess and mother of the last Chinese emperor wasn't enough to protect Youlan, or Princess Chun. When her son misbehaved, Youlan was publicly told off by a wife of the former emperor. This

COURT OF LAW

PRINCESS PROFILE

Anastasia, youngest daughter of the Russian czar, lived in luxury—until 1917. Revolutionaries imprisoned her, along with her parents, brother, and three older sisters. In 1918 the Russian royals were shot dead. But years later, just four skeletons were discovered and rumors started. Had Anastasia and her brother escaped death, after all? The mystery has never been solved.

was too much for her. Youlan drank opium—a drug—and died.

PRINCESSES STILL HAVE TO KEEP ON THE RIGHT SIDE OF PUBLIC OPINION—AND obey the laws of their land.

In some countries, all young people have to do their part for the army—and being a princess isn't a good-enough excuse to wriggle out of it. Even so, royals doing national service probably don't have to clean out the latrines!

Occasionally a princess may get into trouble with the law. Anne, the UK's Princess Royal, was charged with a criminal offense after her English bull terrier, Dotty, attacked two children. The princess was fined and told to get the dog properly trained, much to her relief. The magistrate could have ordered Anne to have Dotty destroyed.

◀ National service is all part of being young and Swedish. Crown Princess Victoria's military training included learning combat skills, shooting, and marching in full gear—camouflaged!

Excuses a princess can make (and what really happened)

♕ **Nobody told me I couldn't. (I'd given my bodyguards the slip.)**

♕ *I didn't realize I was going so fast. (I knew that car could do over 100!)*

♕ **I didn't mean to swear. (I did. The king had just cut my allowance.)**

♕ *I really didn't realize I'd spent so much money. (I deliberately didn't look at any of the price tags.)*

♕ **I didn't touch Mommy's dog and he bit me— perhaps he got stung by something. (Yeah, by my foot.)**

Do Princesses Work?

Most do. It's certainly not the sort of job ordinary people do, with taking a bus to work and a monthly paycheck, but it is work, all the same.

♥ Attending royal events is all part of the job. Crown Princess Maxima of the Netherlands, in a magnificent red flounced gown, arrives at a celebratory concert to mark the Swedish king's sixtieth birthday.

MANY PRINCESSES, WHEN THEY'RE OLD ENOUGH, are expected to take part in ceremonial and state occasions. Lots of people are fascinated by royalty, and the sight of a young princess performing her first public engagement certainly draws in the tourists.

She will also make official visits abroad. These help to promote friendship between countries and to increase trade. Everybody benefits! Princess Ashi Euphelma of Bhutan, who's barely

CHILDREN'S CENTER

in her teens, showed it's never too young to start when she joined her mother on a twelve-day fact-finding visit to India.

Princesses are expected to take part in state occasions

Princesses know that just lending their name to a charity will help to make people aware of the work going on. But many princesses do far more than that. Norway's Crown Princess Mette-Marit spent five days in Malawi investigating the AIDS problem there and visiting the orphaned children who are helped by one of her charities.

A PRINCESS CAN HELP BY SHARING HER PROBLEMS. PRINCESS Beatrice of York made her dyslexia problems public, and now she supports a charity that helps dyslexic children. And in Sweden, Crown Princess Victoria raised awareness for eating disorders when she admitted to having been anorexic.

Having the presence of a princess at a charity ball or dinner immediately helps raise money. The ticket prices are more expensive, and there will certainly be more tickets sold!

♥ **Flags of Thailand and India frame Thai Princess Sirindhorn's face during a two-day visit to India. Her engagements included a World Heritage Site and the Indian Space Research Organization.**

Ways a princess can help a good cause

Make a speech, which is bound to bring publicity.

Support a fund, so others will follow her example.

Attend a ball so the organizers can charge high prices for tickets.

Host a pop concert to attract the rich socialites, A-list celebs—and their checkbooks.

Be photographed cuddling a sick child, then others might stop fearing the child's disease.

Be a good role model: behave, be kind, be fashionable, and be fun!

A princess's job application

Name: *Princess Sane-Jane*

Describe your education:
It went on for a while, but I had a good time, and Mommy says that's what's important.

Any work experience? *Tons! You name it, I've done it— opening things, launching things, naming things... Oh, and lots of meeting and greeting!*

Any interests? *Lots! Clothes, music, films, soaps, adding to my shoe collection, parties, dancing.*

Complete the following: I think I'd be good for this job because...*Daddy says I can do anything I want. And it does sound like fun.*

Princess Professions

Why would a princess have a career of her own? Well, why not? Occasionally it's because she needs the money, but usually it's just because she wants to.

A PRINCESS'S BASIC ROLE IS TO DO A GOOD JOB OF REPRESENTING HER country and to use her position to help others. But sometimes, for one reason or another, it's not enough.

When Princess Märtha Louise married a commoner, she and her Norwegian father agreed that her allowance would be stopped. So she turned to writing children's books to make a living. She went on a US tour to promote her first fairy tale, giving readings in museums, churches, and libraries.

♥ **Princess Märtha Louise tells one of her tales to an audience of children. Her dress was inspired by the story's setting: north Norway's pointy mountains, grassy slopes, and blue seas.**

46

PRINCESS FACT

Russian Princess Olga Alexandrovna nursed wounded soldiers in a World War I hospital.

PRINCESS FACT

In World War II, the UK's Princess Elizabeth learned to strip down an engine.

🔸 Princess Francina Ndimande painted the outside of this Roman Catholic church in South Africa.

The distinctive Ndebele style is bright shapes, outlined in black, on whitewashed walls.

Märtha Louise has also presented her stories on television, on an audio CD, and on the stage in Norway.

Crown Princess Marie-Chantal, of the exiled Greek royal family, has started her own business. She has a designer collection of children's clothes and has opened shops in London, New York, and Greece.

Princess Francina Ndimande has no palace and no great monarchy behind her. She uses her artistic talent to earn her living by house painting—a tradition among Ndebele women. Princess Francina learned her craft as a child, decorating dolls' houses.

PRINCESS ELISABETH OF DENMARK'S LANGUAGE SKILLS (she speaks four languages!) must have been useful in her work for the Danish Ministry of Foreign Affairs. She worked in Denmark, America, and Switzerland—and stayed in the job for forty-five years!

Young or old, princesses find a way to put their talents to good use. Princess Gayatri Devi, of the Jaipur royal family, was once considered one of the world's most beautiful women. She became a politician in her fifties. Now in her eighties, this graceful, elegant lady is helping to promote a line of diamond jewelry.

Sporty Princesses

With access to the best sporting equipment and top instructors, it's no wonder so many princesses are really good at sports.

MANY PRINCESSES ARE INTO SPORTS, BOTH FOR FUN AND TO keep fit. Diana, Princess of Wales, was a regular at her local gym and loved an early morning swim. Swimming's a sport much loved by Princess Mathilde of Belgium and by the Monaco princesses, too.

When princesses get the chance, lots of them head for the ski slopes. Little Catharina-Amalia of the Netherlands enjoys sledding with her sister Alexia— no doubt she'll soon be learning to ski! But Princess Letizia had to learn to ski when she got married, so she could enjoy wintry holidays with other ski-crazy Spanish royals. She'll probably introduce her daughter, Princess Leonor, to the sport as soon as possible. Lucky little Princess

♥ Skiing is one of Princess Elena of Spain's sporting interests—she loves riding, too. Elena's also interested in sports for the disabled. She's a great supporter of the Paralympic Games.

Ingrid of Norway could ask her aunt, Princess Märtha Louise, to teach her to ski. She's a qualified instructor!

MANY PRINCESSES HAD THEIR FIRST EXPERIENCES OF riding on cute family ponies. For some, like Princess Caroline of Monaco's daughter, Charlotte, it began a lifelong love of horses. She's always been crazy about horses and has achieved great show-jumping success, as has Princess Madeleine of Sweden.

Charlotte's achieved great show-jumping success

One of the most famous royal horsewomen is the UK's Princess Royal. Anne's home is the venue for the Gatcombe Park Horse Trials, and she has a distinguished sporting record—the only member of the British royal family to have competed in the Olympic Games! She's given up competition riding but is a patron of lots of horse organizations, notably the Riding for the Disabled Association.

Crown Princess Masako of Japan has taken up horseback riding, as well as tennis, to help improve her health. Princesses, like everyone else, know that exercise is good for you!

◀ **Jordanian Princess Haya was the first female in her country to show jump internationally. She was so good she competed in the Sydney Olympics before turning professional.**

PRINCESS TEASER
What was Spartan Princess Cynisca's claim to equestrian sporting fame? Answer on page 64.

*Princess 1 * *

How to be a princess's perfect pooch

♕

♕ **Bath time? Take it like a champ. You have to smell and look good.**

♕ *Do wag your tail at the king. He needs to be loved.*

♕ **If your portrait is being painted, sit still. Your owner will be in the picture too, and you'll help her relax.**

♕ *Don't bark in the middle of the night. You'll probably wake up about 500 people.*

♕ **Never jump up when the family has visitors. Guests hate hairy clothes.**

♕ *Don't drool. Slobber doesn't look good on the red carpet.*

♠ Nikki, a three-month-old bear, was given to Britain's Princess Anne (now the Princess Royal) in 1956. She donated him to London Zoo.

♠ Princess Haya of Jordan has a soft spot for dogs and horses. This is her favorite Jack Russell terrier.

♥ As a little girl Princess Madeleine of Sweden owned a variety of pets. This cuddlesome rabbit had a harness so its royal owner could take it for walks.

▶ The Princess of Wales (Alexandra of Denmark) with her parrot Cocky in about 1872. She taught him to call out "God save the Queen" if there was a lull in the conversation.

♥ Charlotte of Monaco is a successful horse rider. She competes in events such as show jumping at Fontainebleau in France.

A Girl's Best Friend

When a girl's upset or sad or just feeling lonely, and her parents are away, who does she turn to? Her best friend, of course!

BUT WHEN A PRINCESS WANTS TO CHAT WITH HER BEST FRIEND, she can't just walk through the palace gate and head off to the bus stop, or even next door, without contacting somebody in security. She'll have to wait while a car is brought for her. And there's no doubt that someone in the palace will want to know exactly where she's going and who she'll be seeing. By the time she gets there, she'll probably have cheered up, anyway!

For a princess, a devoted animal can solve the problem. Her pet pooch is always pleased to see her. It doesn't suck up to her just because she's royal. It loves her simply because she is its owner. And it gives her what she needs—complete trust. A princess can whisper secrets into her dog's ear all night long if she wishes, and all it wants in return is the occasional doggie treat.

Dogs have long been popular with princesses. In days gone by, when hygiene wasn't exactly at the forefront of people's minds, dogs were indispensable in castle nurseries as rat-catchers. With their superb sense of hearing, they made good watchdogs, too, and if their owner was ever imprisoned, they were treasured companions.

Most princesses help care for their pets, but they never have to worry about when they go on vacation. There's always someone in a palace to take care of their animals!

Polish exile and model Princess Tamara lets her dog do the work! Cleo models a pricey crystal coat and diamond-studded name tag.

51

Wedding Day: The Dress

Her wedding day is the one day of her life when every girl can be a princess for a few hours. Perhaps she'll even wear a sparkly tiara.

THE BRIDE'S FAMILY AND FRIENDS WILL BE THERE TO SEE HER MARRY the man she loves. There'll be feasting and dancing and laughter and happiness. And the bride will have a photo album to remind her of her magical day.

Planning a wedding is hard work, and there might even be a few tears before the big occasion.

◄ Paparazzi are photographers who will stop at nothing to get the best picture to sell.

1 Mabel of the Netherlands chose bows as the motif for her dress. There were 248 of them.

52

But when a princess gets married, the whole world is

———— ♛ ————

Queen Victoria pioneered the white wedding dress

———————————

watching. On the big day, thousands of photos will be taken, both formal and informal. The paparazzi will be out in full force.

These photographers sell their work to whoever will pay and are all looking for that extra-special picture. Maybe it'll be the one that shows the princess scowling, a smudge on her dress, or even a safety pin doing a vital job.

THE SMART PRINCESS KNOWS SHE HAS TO GET IT RIGHT. SHE MUST look perfect for the public. And what are the people waiting to

♠ **Sketch of the wedding dress for Diana, Princess of Wales, designed by David and Elizabeth Emanuel.**

see? The wedding dress! Queen Victoria pioneered the white wedding dress. Will the bride pick white or a different color? It is bound to be a closely guarded secret, with lots of guesswork. Will it be traditional? Modern?

Dress designers are chosen not just for their skill at making gorgeous clothes but for their ability to keep quiet. Princesses are like all brides the world over. They want everything to be just right. Of course, they have an army of experts to help the day run smoothly, but the dress is their own special choice.

♥ 2 **Sarah of Brunei wore a stunning gold and blue dress topped by a diamond tiara.**

♥ 3 **Princess Noor Hamzah of Jordan chose a beautiful lace mantilla instead of a tiara.**

53

Wedding Guests and Gifts

Every bride fears leaving someone important off the guest list by mistake. Imagine if you were a princess—all those foreign royal relatives to remember, and that's just the beginning...

PRINCESS TEASER

Which prince fell in love with his sister's bridesmaid? Answer on page 64.

A ROYAL WEDDING IS ATTENDED BY WORLD LEADERS, POLITICIANS, members of other royal families and figures of international importance. Then there are those who serve the bride's and groom's families: their servants and office staff. This is a day when they, too, can share the royal limelight. The couple may have showbiz friends—there's often a sprinkling of singers, musicians, comedians, and actors, as well as artists and sports stars. And, of course, there are the friends and family of the bride and groom—those who've loved and supported them as they've grown up.

The majority of guests await the couple in the church, but the most important ones join the

These Japanese people couldn't be guests at Princess Sayako's wedding, but they weren't going to miss a chance to get a glimpse of the bride.

🌢 Crown Princess Mary and her husband, Crown Prince Frederik, received hundreds of gifts from their Danish subjects, including china, silverware, and paintings. They probably never expected His and Hers rugby shirts!

procession. This might be in cars—Princess Sarah of Brunei had 100 limousines in her bridal procession—or in horse-drawn carriages. One of the most unusual processions was Princess Ira von Fürstenberg's in Venice in 1955. She used scarlet, gold, and black gondolas.

WHAT DO YOU GIVE A PRINCESS AS A WEDDING GIFT?

Practically anything! Some people thought Britain's Princess Elizabeth was short of food when she married soon after World War II. She received 500 cases of canned pineapple from Queensland, Australia, and a turkey from an American well-wisher. Mahatma Gandhi sent a length of cloth he'd woven himself. Elizabeth's grandmother was shocked—she thought it was a loincloth! Xenia, daughter of the Russian czar Alexander III, received a fan from her brother. He'd painted a hen, eggs, and baby cockerels on it.

The public can buy souvenirs of the great day. Again, almost anything goes, from tasteful plates and mugs, to odd items, such as cardboard cutouts of the bride and groom with waving hands—or royal wedding soccer balls!

Why do some princesses have boys' names?

👑

When Sophie Rhys-Jones married Prince Edward, she took his title and became The Princess Edward. Since he's also the Earl of Wessex, she's known as the Countess of Wessex, too.

👑

Prince Michael of Kent doesn't have another title, so his wife, Marie-Christine, is known as The Princess Michael.

👑

Kiko of Japan is known as The Princess Akishino, and her cousin Nobuko is known as Princess Tomohito.

👑

Princess Alice of Battenberg married and became Princess Andrew of Greece and Denmark.

👑

Remember Lady Alexandra Duff (on page 6) who dropped the Duff and became a princess? She married a prince and became Princess Arthur!

Prince Joachim of Denmark and his bride Alexandra dance together for the first time as man and wife. Delighted guests clap and close in—until the couple have no room to move!

Feasts, Fun, and Flowers

A princess wants just the same features at her wedding as any bride. The difference is that royal ceremonies are usually bigger and better!

A ROYAL WEDDING RECEPTION IS A LARGE, COSTLY AFFAIR, although not many reach the scale of Princess Sarah of Brunei's extravaganza—a feast for literally thousands! But when Napoleon married Marie Louise, the daughter of Francis I of Austria, in 1810, the couple treated all the well-wishers outside to one of the first-ever street barbecues. They served charcoal-roasted lamb and sausages.

Princess Elizabeth's postwar wedding reception was limited to family, close friends, and courtiers. They did it in style,

though—guests ate from gold plates while bagpipes played. Even more low-key was the marriage of Princess Rym of Jordan in 2004. Money that might have

Princess Mathilde had 25,000 flowers in the church

been spent on a lavish reception was used instead to help the poor.

The real showstopper of any wedding feast is the cake. If all the guests will taste it, it has to be large. Sometimes it's a good idea to have more than one cake. When the Prince of Wales married Camilla Parker-Bowles in 2005, Buckingham Palace ordered twenty cakes!

FLOWERS MAKE ANY WEDDING LOOK SPECIAL, BUT PRINCESSES need more than most. The procession route must be decorated, as well as the church and reception. In Belgium, Princess Mathilde had 25,000 flowers in the church alone. Her sister-in-law, Princess Claire, was surrounded by great banks of white blooms when she married Prince Laurent in 2003.

It's the bridal bouquet that everyone notices. In a break from tradition,

Norwegian Crown Princess Mette-Marit carried a long garland of purple and white flowers over her wrist. Princess Mary of Denmark included eucalyptus in her bouquet, from her native Australia. British royal bouquets always contain a sprig of myrtle. It's picked from a bush grown from a sprig in the bridal bouquet of Princess Vicky—Queen Victoria's eldest daughter.

▶ **For her May wedding, Letizia of Spain carried a bouquet of scented white roses, apple blossom, lilies, and lily of the valley. It also included stalks of wheat for fertility.**

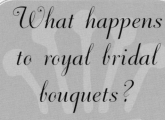

What happens to royal bridal bouquets?

♛ **Princess Kalina of Bulgaria gave her bouquet, flower by flower, to the people who stood outside the church singing folk songs for her.**

♛ Crown Princess Mary of Denmark's bouquet was taken to Scotland, by her aunt, to be laid on Mary's mother's grave.

♛ **Another Princess Mary, daughter of George V of England, stopped on the way back from her wedding in 1922 to lay her flowers at the Cenotaph, a war memorial in London.**

♛ Princess Sarah of Brunei's bouquet probably wasn't allowed to stray too far from the royal vaults. Instead of flowers, it was made of gold, diamonds, and other precious stones!

Darling Mom,

I love it here at West Heath. A girl named Diana is looking out for me. She's super fun! Anything for a dare! In class I offered my sour candies and she ate five at once. She did!

She's awfully kind, especially to animals. She wants to be a preschool teacher. Most of us want to travel and get married, so that'll probably be the last we'll hear of her. Oh! Diana has put on a ballet skirt and riding hat! She's up to something and I don't want to miss it.

Luv'n'hugs,
Arabella

Diana: Lady to Princess

Quiet, shy Diana Spencer's destiny was to marry the heir to the British throne. She became one of the most beautiful women in the world and the most famous princess of all.

DIANA SPENCER'S FAMILY LIVED ON ONE OF THE QUEEN'S estates, so she was no stranger to royalty. Princes Andrew and Edward came to play with her! Sadly, Diana's parents split up and her mother moved to London.

When Diana went to West Heath boarding school, she didn't exactly throw herself into schoolwork, and she hardly managed to pass any exams.

➤ **Prince Charles and nineteen-year-old Diana laugh together on the day their engagement is announced to the world. Her blue suit perfectly matches the huge sapphire in her engagement ring.**

PRINCESS FACT
When Diana was young, her family nickname was "Duch"—short for "Duchess."

However, she loved activities such as ballet and won trophies for swimming and diving. She also made lasting friendships.

WHEN DIANA'S GRANDFATHER DIED, HER FATHER became Earl Spencer, she became Lady Diana Spencer, and the family moved to their ancestral home, Althorp.

It was in a field at Althorp that Diana, in rain boots, was introduced to twenty-eight-year-old Charles, Prince of Wales. She was sixteen. Did romance blossom? Not a bit. Charles was already dating Diana's sister.

Eventually, Diana moved to London. She shared an apartment with her girlfriends and worked as a preschool assistant. She went to lots of parties and dances and saw more and more of Prince Charles. She fell deeply in love, and when he proposed, she said yes, thinking she would one day become his queen.

The press and public fell in love with the sweet girl with huge eyes and a shy smile. The royal family was delighted, too. Diana came from an aristocratic background—she was descended from Charles I—so she was the perfect bride for Charles.

PRINCESS FACT
Before going out with Prince Charles, Diana worked as a cleaning lady!

 Diana loved animals and had lots of pets. Her Shetland pony, Soufflé, clearly loved her as much as she loved him!

♥ The world watched Diana step from the glass coach in her fairy-tale wedding dress. She went into the cathedral a lady and came out a princess: Diana, Princess of Wales!

♥ Diana's black gown is enhanced by her jewels: diamond and sapphire crescent earrings, with matching necklace and bracelet. The tiara is the one she wore on her wedding day.

Diana: Queen of Hearts

After their fairy-tale wedding and a honeymoon on the royal yacht Britannia, everything seemed perfect for Diana and her prince. But would they live happily ever after?

LESS THAN A YEAR AFTER THE WEDDING, PRINCE WILLIAM WAS BORN. Charles and Diana were thrilled. He was the heir who'd follow his father to the throne. Two years later, Diana gave birth to Prince Harry. Now the royal family had an heir and a "spare."

Diana went on royal tours and performed public engagements, both with her husband and alone. The public adored her. She went from teenager to elegant young woman and developed her own style. She became a glamorous icon. Her face on a magazine cover guaranteed greatly increased sales. Diana couldn't go anywhere without the flash of cameras. At times it upset her, but she was famous and beautiful and everyone wanted pictures of her.

Then came dark days. Charles and Diana's marriage fell apart. There were many reasons, but a long-standing one was Charles's relationship with Camilla Parker-Bowles, which began before he met Diana. They were still close. The unthinkable happened. The Prince and Princess of Wales divorced.

 Tributes left by the grieving public formed an ocean of flowers, candles, teddy bears, and messages outside the gates of Diana's home, Kensington Palace.

DIANA KNEW NOW THAT SHE'D NEVER BE THE COUNTRY'S queen. But she felt she could be a queen of people's hearts. She'd always been committed to many charities, and she was quick to comfort the sick or unhappy. She devoted herself to helping others, especially people living with AIDS and people at risk from landmines.

On the night of August 31, 1997, Diana was riding in a car through Paris. The car entered a tunnel and crashed. Diana died that night.

The nation was shocked beyond belief. Its beautiful princess was gone. A week later, people grieved at her funeral. William and Harry followed their mother's coffin.

People comforted themselves by believing that Diana lives on in her sons. One day Prince William will marry, and his bride will become the next princess.

 Diana visited a landmined site in Angola and spent time with children who'd lost limbs.
The resulting publicity highlighted the terrible injuries landmines inflict, long after a war is over.

Diana's days off

Some of Diana's happiest days were spent doing ordinary things. William and Harry enjoyed...

 Getting drenched on a water ride

 Eating burgers and ice cream

 Going to the movies

 Visiting the theater with friends

 Building sand castles on the beach

 Having fun in the snow

...and Diana was with them every time.

British Princesses

Whether they were British-born or left their homelands to marry into the UK's royal family, British princesses have a proud history—with a few exceptions!

Unhappy endings

♔ **Princess Caroline's** husband, George IV, didn't invite her to his coronation. They'd had a falling out years before. When she tried to get into Westminster Abbey, burly guards blocked her way. Caroline died less than three weeks later.

♔ *Princess Isabella was married to Edward II but fell in love with an earl, Roger Mortimer. They overthrew the king and even plotted his murder. Isabella's son, Edward III, had Mortimer executed but spared his mother. She was sent to live in Norfolk.*

♔ **Prince William and his half sister, Matilda, went to sea on the brand-new *White Ship*. Their father, King Henry I, sailed on another vessel. The *White Ship* struck a rock and capsized. The children, along with almost everyone on board, drowned.**

Died AD 60/61 Boudicca's daughters
When Queen Boudicca waged war against the Romans, her two princesses went with her. They lost the war, and no one knows how they died.

1080–1118 Princess Edith
Edith of Scotland married Henry I and was crowned Queen Matilda. She befriended lepers—outcasts of society—and washed and kissed their feet.

1241–1290 Eleanor of Castile
When Eleanor died, her body was taken from Lincoln to London. Later, her husband, Edward I of England, put up memorials called "Eleanor crosses" along the route.

1485–1536 Catherine of Aragon
Katherine married her brother-in-law! When her husband, the Prince of Wales, died, she was married off to his brother, who became Henry VIII.

1496–1533 Princess Mary Tudor
Henry VIII was fond of his sister, Mary. He named his first daughter after her and also his best warship—the *Mary Rose*.

1516–1558 Princess Mary Tudor
When Henry's daughter Mary became queen, she burned hundreds of people at the stake for refusing to follow her religion— and earned the nickname "Bloody Mary."

PRINCESS FACT
The Princess Royal is a licensed truck driver. She's also driven a tank!

1596–1662 Princess Elizabeth Stuart
The Gunpowder Plot conspirators planned to kidnap nine-year-old Elizabeth, kill her father, King James I, and make her queen.

1665–1714 Anne of Denmark
Anne followed her father, James II, to the English throne.

1744–1818 Princess Charlotte
When Charlotte married George III, she was the first queen to ride in the same gold state coach that's now used for coronations.

1819–1901 Princess Victoria
Victoria had to sleep with her mother throughout her childhood. Once she became queen she put an end to that. She had a room of her own!

1833–1897 Princess Mary Adelaide
Mary, granddaughter of George III, had expensive tastes. She and her husband ran up huge bills and fled to Italy to escape the debt collectors.

1843–1878 Princess Alice
Queen Victoria's third child, Alice, was nicknamed "Fatima" for being a bit tubby. Grand Duke Louis IV of Hesse didn't care. He married her and they had seven children!

1848–1939 Princess Louise
Victoria's sixth child, Louise, was hurt in an accident in Canada just before her thirty-second birthday. Her sleigh overturned! Luckily she recovered and lived to ninety-one.

1867–1931 Louise, Princess Royal
Edward VII's daughter, Louise, was shipwrecked with her family off the Moroccan coast. Everyone struggled to shore but a few weeks later, her husband, the Duke of Fife, died.

PRINCESS FACT
Princess Michael was known as "Princess Pushy" because of her regal ways.

1869–1938 Princess Maud of Wales
Louise's tomboyish sister, Maud—nicknamed "Harry"—married Danish Prince Carl. When he was offered a kingship, Maud unexpectedly found herself queen of Norway!

1872–1956 Princess Marie Louise
Queen Victoria's granddaughter Marie Louise created a magnificent doll's house for Queen Mary. It had lights, running water—and a throne!

1876–1936 Princess Victoria
Known as "Ducky" to her family, Victoria was another of Queen Victoria's grandchildren. She caused a scandal in the early twentieth century when she divorced her first husband, a German prince, and married a Russian grand duke.

Born 1926 Princess Elizabeth
Princess Elizabeth, now Queen, made a wartime wireless broadcast with her sister, Princess Margaret, to cheer up evacuees missing their parents.

1930–2002 Princess Margaret Rose
When Margaret wanted to be a Brownie, a pack was started at Buckingham Palace. At first, Brownies wore their best dresses instead of uniforms!

Born 1936 Princess Alexandra
The Queen's cousin, Alexandra, was the first British princess to attend an ordinary school. She'd barely begun when she took time off—to be Princess Elizabeth's bridesmaid.

Born 1950 The Princess Royal
Anne, once called "Princess Sourpuss," showed her jokey side when she appeared on a TV quiz show. She hit her team captain with her handbag!

Born 1988 Princess Beatrice of York
"Bea," as she's known, has a startling birth date. She was born at eighteen minutes past eight, on August 8, 1988. That can be written as 8:18, 8/8/88!

Born 1990 Princess Eugenie of York
and her sister Princess Beatrice of York are the only granddaughters of the Queen to hold the title of Princess.

PRINCESS FACT
Princess Elizabeth had a honeymoon for three! She took her corgi, Susan.

Index

Answers to Princess Teasers

p. 13 mr: Aiko of Japan was visiting Tokyo Disneyland.

p. 13 br: Phuwiangosaurus sirindhornae was named after Sirindhorn of Thailand.

p. 19: Elizabeth, now queen of the UK; she was in a treetop hotel in Africa when her father died.

p. 24: Elizabeth Tudor, later Elizabeth I of England.

p. 25: Charles I's daughter, Elizabeth, during the English Civil War.

p. 35: Stephanie of Monaco.

p. 38: Crown Princess Mary of Denmark.

p. 39: Beatrice and Eugenie's mom, Sarah, Duchess of York.

p. 49: She was the first woman to have a win at the ancient Olympics. She owned the horses—women weren't allowed to compete.

p. 54: Constantine of Greece wanted to dance with no one else but Princess Anne-Marie of Denmark at his sister's wedding.